HISTORY QUICK READ NO. 7

Stories of the Saxons and Vikings

By David Oakden

Illustrated by Stephen Millingen

a
ANGLIA *young* BOOKS

First published in 1995
by Anglia Young Books
Durhams Farmhouse
Ickleton
Saffron Walden, Essex CB10 1SR

Illustrations by Stephen Millingen

British Library Cataloguing-in-Publication Data
A catalogue record for this book is available from the
British Library

ISBN 1 871173 43 4

Typeset in Sassoon Primary by Goodfellow & Egan,
Cambridge and printed in Great Britain by Ashford Press,
Curdridge, Southampton

CONTENTS

THE LAST JOURNEY
AD 625

The boat was long and beautiful.
The front end curved upwards to a
carved <u>dragon's head</u>. It would take
40 men to row this boat. But there
were no oars. There was no sail.
There was no mast.

A man called Sigbert had made the
boat. Sigbert lived near the village

of Sutton. Now he stood looking at the boat with his daughter Gwen.

'It's a beautiful boat, Father,' said Gwen. 'But why is it on dry land? Where is the sail? Why was it made so quickly?'

Sigbert said, 'This boat does not need a sail. It will never go on water. It is for King Redwald.'

'But King Redwald is dead,' said Gwen.

'Yes,' said Sigbert. 'That is why I had to make it quickly. He is to be buried in this boat. Tomorrow is the funeral.'

Thunder rumbled out at sea and lightning flashed. It had been very hot that day, but it had not rained.

Everywhere was dry. The grass was dry, trees were dry and the river Deben had only a little water in it.

Gwen slept badly that night. Rag the dog lay near her. It was hot so the house door was wide open. A vivid flash of lightning woke Gwen up and made Rag growl.

Gwen got up and crept out of the house. Rag followed. Outside it was still very hot and the storm was close. But it had not rained.

Another flash of lightning lit up the village. In the distance Gwen saw the boat, standing tall, waiting. But now a dry wind came, picking up dust and scattering it against her bare legs.

The wind got stronger. Gwen wondered about the boat. Suppose the wind blew it over. 'Come on, Rag,' she whispered. 'Let's go and have a look.'

She ran in her bare feet, Rag with her. When they got to the boat she stopped worrying. Ten strong wooden poles were holding the boat upright.

Lightning flashed again and there was a crash of thunder. Dry leaves swirled all round her. Gwen sniffed. Something, somewhere was burning. There was a red glow over in the woods. The lightning had struck a

tree and set it on fire. As Gwen watched, flames suddenly shot up into the air. Another tree caught fire. A gust of wind blew smoke and sparks towards her.

Gwen felt a spark on her bare leg. She bent down to rub it off. But then there was another, and another. Soon the air was full of sparks and a crackling, roaring sound was coming from the woods.

Gwen gasped. A little fire had started by her feet. A spark must have landed in dry leaves. Gwen stamped it out and then shouted. Her bare foot was burnt.

Two more little fires started. The dry grass was burning. Gwen thought,

'The boat! It will catch fire. I must run to the village for help.'

But it was too late. By the time she got to the village the boat would be burnt to ashes. She would have to stay and put the fires out.

Then she thought of Rag the dog. He could fetch help 'Run, Rag!' she shouted. 'Go and fetch your master.' Rag wagged his tail but did not go. 'Run, you stupid dog!' she yelled.

Then something happened that made Rag go. A burning twig fell near him and a spark landed on his tail. Rag did not wait any longer. He howled and set off for home.

Gwen was alone. As she stood there a shower of sparks and blazing twigs fell near her. A lot of little fires started. Now smoke was coming from inside the boat.

A plank was leaning against the boat. Gwen climbed up it. A fire was burning near the back. It was too big to stamp out.

She looked round. Her father's work-shirt was lying in the boat. Gwen picked it up and started to beat out the fire with it.

Sparks flew everywhere and black smoke got in her eyes and throat. Gwen started to cry. She beat and beat at the flames. But then another fire started at the front of the boat. The dragon's head was lit up by the flames.

'Help!' Gwen yelled. 'Help me!
Please help!'

Suddenly there were voices. Men
came running. They climbed up the
sides of the boat. Buckets of water
were thrown. There were loud
hissing noises and the flames went
out.

Sigbert held Gwen in his arms,
hugging her. They were both crying.
'Rag woke me,' said Sigbert. 'Thank
God we were in time. You are safe
and the boat is safe.'

Gwen's mother washed and
bandaged Gwen's legs and feet. Men
and women scrubbed the smoke
stains off the boat. The burnt wood
was scraped clean. New paint went
on the dragon's head.

Soon it was morning and time for King Redwald's funeral. A large crowd gathered. The King's body was lifted into the boat and placed in an open coffin. A priest said a prayer. A trumpet blew a sad note.

'Now what will happen?' said Gwen.

'Watch,' said Sigbert. 'Look at that.'

All kinds of wonderful things were being put into the boat. First went the King's <u>helmet</u> with pictures of fighting men on it. Next came his sword with jewels in the <u>hilt</u>. Then a bundle of spears, a <u>battle-axe</u> and a shield were put near the dead King.

'The weapons will keep him safe on his journey to the next world,' said Sigbert.

Next to go in were some <u>drinking horns</u> with silver bands, a great silver bowl and some silver spoons. 'Now he will be able to eat and drink on his journey,' said Sigbert.

Gwen said, 'Look, Father! Jewels!'

A heap of jewels was piled on the dead King's chest. There was silver and gold and a bag of coins. Last of all was the King's belt with a <u>buckle</u> made of solid gold. The buckle had a design of snakes and animals all twisted together.

The trumpet blew again. Men with spades began to cover the boat with

soil. They went on working all day. By nightfall, they had made a large mound. The boat was buried under it.

'A dead king is in our boat,' said Gwen. 'I can hardly believe it.'

'Yes,' said Sigbert. 'Thanks to you. If you had not got up in the night the boat would have burned.'

'If Rag hadn't fetched you it would have burned anyway,' said Gwen.

'Yes, we must thank you both,' said Sigbert. 'But now King Redwald is going on his last journey. It is time for people like us to get on with our lives.'

And with their arms round each
other they walked back to their
breakfasts.

GLOSSARY

battle-axe
an axe used in fighting

buckle
a metal fastening on a belt

burial mound
a small hill, made by men, used to bury important people when they died

dragon's head
the front end of a boat was often carved into the shape of a dragon or a god

drinking horn
a cow's horn, used as a wine-cup

helmet
a metal hat, worn in battle

hilt
The handle of a sword or battle-axe

HISTORICAL NOTES for THE LAST JOURNEY

It was an old Viking tradition to bury important people in a boat with weapons and food and jewels. The boat was supposed to take them on their journey to the next world. The weapons were to protect them on that journey. The food was to eat on the way.

Sutton Hoo is near the River Deben in Suffolk. There are seventeen <u>burial mounds</u> there, some of them still not dug out. The mound in the story was uncovered in 1939.

No actual body was found in the boat, but there was the outline of a coffin. So nobody knows for sure who was buried there. It may have been King Redwald who died in AD

625: we know about him from a history book written by a monk called Bede.

The armour and treasures mentioned in the story were all found there. They are now in the British Museum in London. There were nineteen pieces of jewellery, including a gold buckle weighing nearly a pound and a purse holding forty coins.

EELS FOR KING OFFA
AD 781

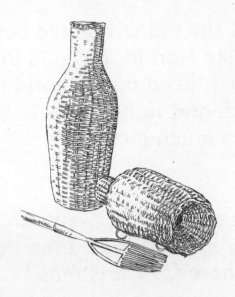

There was a new mill in Tamworth. It had fine new grind-stones and its great wheel was turned by the rushing water of the River Anker. 'It could grind all the corn in <u>Mercia</u>,' said Edward the miller.

The mill door opened. Harold, King

Offa's <u>steward</u>, stood there. 'Good day, miller,' he said.

Edward the miller nodded coldly. He didn't like Harold. Nobody in Tamworth liked him. Harold was very rich and nobody knew how he made so much money.

'It is December the twentieth,' said Harold. 'In four days' time the King will be here for Christmas.'

Edward nodded again. 'I am ready,' he said.

'You had better be,' said Harold. 'This year I want bread for the King, his family, three chiefs and three bishops. Then there are all the officials and <u>abbots</u> and other visitors.'

'There will plenty of flour,' said Edward.

The steward unrolled a paper. It said:

'Food needed for the Feast of St. Stephen, the day after Christmas Day, in the Year of Our Lord 781:

10 jars of honey	20 hens
300 loaves	10 cheeses
42 <u>casks</u> of ale	1 cask of butter
2 old <u>oxen</u>	5 salmon
10 geese	100 eels'

Edward said, 'All that, just for one meal?'

'All that,' said Harold the steward. 'You must provide flour for the 300 loaves. But that is not all. Seth the

eel-fisher is ill, so you must also get the eels.'

Harold went away. Edward was very worried. He said, 'Where can I get 100 eels? The river is almost frozen over. There is ice on the ponds.'

'Can't the King eat dried salt-fish?' said Sara, Edward's daughter.

Edward groaned. 'Don't be silly. If there are no eels I shall be in trouble. This mill belongs to King Offa. The steward will be quick to tell him that I am no good. The King will turn us out.'

Sara said, 'Father, we can't be turned out just for a few eels.' She walked into the town. Up above her

was a great mound, like a flat-
topped hill. The King's hall and the
church were up there. Down below
were the houses and shops. Sara
went to a poor house near the
market. It was the house of Seth the
eel-fisher.

The house had only one room. Seth
the eel-fisher was lying on a straw
bed in one corner, coughing.

'I am sorry you are ill,' said Sara.

Seth's wife said, 'He has the fever. I
have given him hot <u>coltsfoot</u> and
honey, but his chest is bad.'

'How can we get 100 eels for the
King?' asked Sara.

Seth said in a weak voice, 'Don't worry. I have put the traps in the river. Just find them and empty them.' He told Sara where the traps were.

Sara ran down to the river. The water was icy, but Sara waded in. She put her hands under the water and felt a rope. She pulled and a long basket came out of the water. The basket looked like a big straw bottle. She took it onto the grass and tipped it up. Twenty eels slid out.

'Eels!' she shouted, but they started to slide back into the water. She grabbed at them but most of them got away. She was left with just two.

Sara waded in again. There was another rope and another basket. This time she took more care, but in the end she only had fifteen eels.

She set the traps again and went home. But next day there were no eels at all. Seth said, 'You set the traps the wrong way. They must face downstream. Fish always swim upstream.'

Next day was Christmas Eve. Sara caught twenty more eels. But there was no more time. Sara's mother put the eels in a pot and cooked them on the fire. Then she pickled them in salt and vinegar. They smelt good.

'There are not many,' she said. 'You must tell Harold that this is the best we can do.'

On St. Stephen's morning, Sara set off. It was still dark. As she came to the market, she saw a cart pulled by two oxen. Harold the steward was standing by the cart, talking to the driver. 'Have you got the ale?' said the steward.

'Yes', said the driver. 'I have taken 25 casks up to the hall. These are the other five.'

The steward said, 'Good. King Offa wants these five to be put in my brother's house. Follow me.'

Sara thought, 'That's funny.' She kept in the shadows and followed them. They came to a house and started to carry in the casks of ale. Sara crept up and took a look

inside. She gasped. The house was full of food!

There were sides of meat hanging from the roof. There was a big bowl of eggs in one corner and three sacks of flour in another. A cask of butter lay on its side. Four geese and a salmon were on the table.

Sara ran up the hill to the King's hall. Everybody was rushing about. A servant said, 'Good. You have got the eels. Wait here until the feast has started.'

Time went slowly, but at last the servant pushed Sara into the great hall. It was warm and full of people eating and drinking. A man was singing and playing on pipes. A juggler was juggling. Dogs were chewing bones. Servants were rushing round with food and drink. There was a strong smell of meat and ale.

'Eels!' shouted King Offa. Sara went up with the dish. King Offa looked at it. 'What a few!' he said.

The steward was there. He grabbed Sara's arm and pinched it. 'This is a lazy family,' he said. 'Her father is the miller. He cheats people with his measures. He puts sand in his flour.'

Sara said, 'He does not.' But King Offa said, 'If he cheats, get rid of him. Bring more ale!'

The steward said, 'Lord, it has all gone. There is no more in the town. I can get some for tomorrow, but I shall need more money to pay for it.'

The King reached for his purse, but Sara remembered the five casks of ale on the cart. She said, 'Lord, I know where there are five more of your casks.'

'What!' laughed the King. 'Does she know more than our steward? Go with her, Brorda and fetch this ale.'

Brorda the chief stood up. His eyes twinkled. 'It had better be good ale,' he said. 'Where is it?'

Sara said, 'The steward hid it in the town. There are other things there

33

as well. Butter and geese and eggs and ... and ...' her voice tailed off as the King got to his feet. His face was red with anger.

Suddenly everybody stopped talking. The King took hold of Harold by the throat. 'Is this true?' he said. 'Are you cheating me?'

The steward fell to his knees. A soldier took him away. Then men went to the house and brought back the food and ale.

Ten days later King Offa left Tamworth. 'He has gone West to where the Welshmen are raiding our lands,' said Edward the miller. 'He is going to build a great <u>dyke</u> to keep the Welshmen out. The dyke will stretch from the river Dee in the north to the river Wye in the south.'

Sara said, 'Never mind King Offa's dyke. What about our mill? What has happened to Harold, the steward?'

'Harold has gone,' said Edward. 'He may be dead. Men who cheat the King have short lives. But thanks to you we shall keep the mill.' He put his arm round her. 'You may not be good at catching slippery eels, but you caught a slippery steward!'

GLOSSARY

abbot
the chief monk in an abbey

cask
a wooden barrel

coltsfoot
a small plant with yellow flowers

dyke
a ditch and mound of earth, made to keep enemies out

Mercia
old Anglo-Saxon kingdom in the middle and South of
Britain

oxen
cows, used for milking, pulling carts and for eating.

steward
an important man, in charge of the King's household

HISTORICAL NOTES for EELS FOR KING OFFA

Tamworth, a town now in Staffordshire, was an important place in King Offa's time. It was where he always spent Easter and Christmas. His palace there was 100 feet long, with wall paintings, a high roof, gold-painted seats and rich tapestries. It stood on a high mound and had its own chapel nearby. There was a ditch all round it. The ditch had sharp stakes facing outwards to keep off enemies.

A mill was a very important building. The new mill at Tamworth had an upstairs as well as a ground floor. It was unusual because it had glass windows, steel bearings and two huge grind stones brought over from Germany.

Eels were a favourite fish to eat. An eel-basket is shaped like a big straw bottle. Bait is put in it. The eels swim in through the narrow end, but they cannot find their way out again.

Offa's Dyke was completed in about 787 AD. It marked the border between England and Wales. It was 25 feet deep and 150 miles long. About 80 miles of it are still standing.

THE VIKING BOY
AD 991

It was a fine, warm day in the town of Hedeby in Denmark. Rolf was going for a swim in the river with his friends, but he heard a shout.

'Rolf! I need you.' It was his mother. Rolf turned and went inside the house. It was a big house, made of split logs standing on end. Cracks between the logs were plastered with mud to keep out the cold. The roof was covered with <u>turf</u>. The house had three rooms.

A fire burned inside the big room. An iron cooking-pot hung over the flames.

Rolf's mother said, 'The new stones for my weaving <u>loom</u> are ready. Your father put them in the fire last night to make them hard. This morning he took them out and they are now cold. Please fix them on the loom for me. I want to weave a new shawl.'

The loom stood against the wall. The stones were balls of clay with a hole through the middle. They had to be tied to the ends of the long threads. The weight of the stones pulled the threads straight.

As Rolf was working, his father Trig came in. he had a <u>helmet</u> in his hand. It was round and had pieces to protect his nose and eyes.

'Trig!' said his wife. 'Why have you got your helmet?'

Trig took a battle-axe from a hook. The axe was broad and sharp. He looked at his wife. 'The King sails tomorrow,' he said. 'I shall go with him. We are going to the land called England.'

Rolf said, 'I am nearly a man now. Can I go too?'

'No,' said his mother. 'You are too young.'

But Trig looked at his son. 'You are young,' he said. 'You do not know how to fight yet. But I will take you. You must learn how to be a man.'

Next day everybody went down to the <u>harbour</u>. King Olaf was there with ninety-three ships. Trig's ship was one of them. It was sixty feet long. It curved upwards at each end and there were benches for fifty men.

Hundreds of men were getting on the ships. Their wives and families stood around. The men would be away for many months.

They loaded food and drink. The men had swords, battle-axes and

spears. They hung their painted shields on the side of the ships.

King Olaf gave an order. Square sails were hoisted and the fleet moved away from Hedeby.

Rolf stood at the back of the ship, waving until he could see land no more. The sea was rough. Rolf was sick again and again. But after some days, they saw the flat lands of England.

'I know this place,' said King Olaf. 'There is a town near here called Maldon. Run the boats on the beach.'

A strong wind was blowing and the waves were very big. There was white foam on them. Then disaster struck! As Trig's boat got close to the beach a big wave broke over it.

'Help!' screamed Rolf. The wave had knocked him off the boat. He was in the sea. Another wave came and he went under. Salt water was in his mouth and nose.

Then he felt strong arms round him. Trig had jumped in to save him. They struggled to the beach.

Trig's boat was still close to the beach. It was coming for them. Then they heard a noise behind them. A band of Saxons was running through the sand-dunes, waving bows and swords.

The Saxons started to fire arrows at the boats. The Danes had to sail away. Trig and Rolf were left on the beach and taken prisoner.

'Don't kill the boy!' shouted Trig. One of the Saxons took Trig's sword and axe.

'Be brave,' said Trig to Rolf. 'King Olaf will come back for us. He will not leave us here.'

They were taken across some <u>mudflats</u> to the town of Maldon. They were kept in a hut for three days and nights. They slept on damp straw and ate bread and water.

Then Britnoth, the Saxon chief, sent for them.

'Your friends have been raiding our lands up the coast,' said Britnoth to Trig. 'But now they have landed on an island. That is a mistake. We can stop them at the <u>causeway</u> before they reach the mainland.'

'What is a causeway?' said Rolf to his father.

'It is a narrow strip of land,' said Trig. 'At low tide you can walk across from the island to the mainland. But at high tide it is covered by the sea. A few men can hold off an army there.'

Trig turned to Britnoth. 'You are right,' he said. 'You can hold them off at the causeway. But one day you will have to fight us. Why not let them cross the causeway now and settle things for good?'

The chief rubbed his beard. 'You are right,' he said at last. 'Only a battle will settle things. I will let your men cross the causeway. Then we shall be able to kill them all. None of them will escape.'

He gave an order. 'What did he say?' asked Rolf. Trig said, 'He is going to send us back to King Olaf with a message. I can hardly believe it.'

Rolf and Trig were taken to the causeway. The tide was going out. Soon they would be able to cross.

'Go across to the island,' said Britnoth. 'Tell your King that Saxons will fight and die for their land. Tomorrow we will let your men cross the causeway. Then there can be a fair fight on dry land.'

At first King Olaf did not trust the message. He thought it was a trap. But there were no Saxons near the causeway. The Danes marched across and set up camp on the mainland.

Next morning the Saxons attacked. The battle lasted all day. At first King Olaf's men were pressed back towards the sea. Many Danes were killed.

But Olaf waved his battle-axe over his head. 'Follow me!' he roared. 'Kill their chief!' He chopped down two Saxons and his men charged after him.

Britnoth was a mighty man and a great fighter, but the Danes got closer. King Olaf fought like a madman. Dead bodies lay all round him.

At last Britnoth was struck with a spear and fell dead.

The Saxons had lost their leader. Some of them ran away. Before long it was all over. The Danes had won.

All this time Rolf had been waiting near the boats. Now he ran to find Trig. The sight of the dead men upset him. 'So many dead,' he cried. Trig put his arm round him. 'Men who die in battle go to live with the gods. We will bury them with their weapons.'

The Saxons said they would pay King Olaf money if he stopped raiding their lands. There would be peace and some of the Danes could settle in England.

Britnoth the Saxon Chief was dead, but his wife was still alive. 'I loved my husband,' she said, weeping. 'He was a brave man and a good chief. I will make a <u>tapestry</u> about him and the battle of Maldon.'

Some days later Trig and Rolf sailed back to Hedeby. In time Rolf grew to be a man. He took part in many more raids. He became a mighty warrior. But he never forgot the battle that took place after the soldiers had crossed the causeway near Maldon.

GLOSSARY

causeway
a path joining an island to the mainland. The causeway at Maldon was covered with water at high tide

harbour
where boats can be loaded and unloaded

helmet
a metal hat, worn in battle

loom
a frame for weaving cloth

mùd-flats
flat land, often covered by the sea at low tide

sand-dunes
small hills of sand near a beach, made by the waves

tapestry
a picture made by needlework, often showing a story rather like a strip cartoon

turf
pieces of grassy soil

HISTORICAL NOTES for THE VIKING BOY

The Battle of Maldon was fought in AD 991. The King of Norway, Olaf Tryggvason, attacked the east coast of England. He burned the town of Ipswich. At Maldon on 10th August, he was met by the Saxon chief Britnoth.

The Danes landed near Maldon on Northey Island. Britnoth and the Saxon army were on the mainland, with a narrow causeway between them and the Danes. The Danes tried to cross the causeway, but it was so narrow that a handful of Saxons were able to stop them.

At last the Danes asked the Saxons to let them across so that they could fight on dry land. The Saxons did so, probably because they thought they could beat the Danes and so get rid of them for ever. But the Saxons lost and Britnoth was killed. The Danes took control of that part of the country and made the Saxons pay heavy taxes in gold and silver.

When it was all over, Britnoth's widow made a tapestry about the battle of Maldon. There is also a famous Anglo-Saxon poem, written about 40 years later, which tells how Britnoth died fighting, like a hero.